D1162801

MAURICE UTRILLO

Maurice Utrillo. V.

by Jeanine Warnod

COLLECTOR'S EDITION
BOUND IN GENUINE LEATHER

The Easton Press
NORWALK, CONNECTICUT

Translated from the French by:
INA LEE SELDEN

Collection published under the direction of:
MADELEINE LEDIVELEC-GLOECKNER

© 1983 BONFINI PRESS CORPORATION, NAEFELS, SWITZERLAND
TRANSLATION COPYRIGHT © 1983 BY INA LEE SELDEN
ALL RIGHTS OF REPRODUCTION OF ILLUSTRATIONS BY S.P.A.D.E.M., PARIS
ALL RIGHTS IN THE U.S.A. ARE RESERVED BY CROWN PUBLISHERS, INC., NEW YORK, NEW YORK

THE SPECIAL CONTENTS OF THIS EDITION ARE COPYRIGHT© 1983
BY THE EASTON PRESS, NORWALK, CONNECTICUT

Title page: Suzanne Valadon
PORTRAIT OF MAURICE UTRILLO, 1921
Oil on canvas, 26″ × 20½″ (66 × 52 cm)
Private collection

QUAY IN PARIS, 1905–06. Oil on canvas, $14^{15}/_{16}'' \times 17^{11}/_{16}''$ (38 × 45 cm) Private collection

Maurice Utrillo's work never fails to move me. The day I was born he gave me a painting of a simple church in a village of the Loiret. The church was of no particular style or period and had no special character. It was surrounded by a few ordinary buhrstone houses set on an endless country road. Next to his signature, «Maurice Utrillo, V,» he added in a hesitant script, «To Mademoiselle Jeanine Warnod.» The gift was a token of appreciation for my father, who had championed Utrillo's work.[1]

_____

(1) See page 79.

I would like to strip Utrillo of his legend and show the true face of this sensitive, isolated, unhappy artist, seated before his masterpieces muttering, «Not ordinary, not at all ordinary.» I would like to show the unknown side of this doomed figure, this character out of a novel whom Montmartre considered an inveterate drunkard. The anecdotes, now twisted out of recognition, make a mockery of an engaging artist and his work. And his work, after all, is the only witness to his genius.

Who is Maurice Utrillo, V?

He defies categories. He fits into no school. In the history of art, his place is among artists led by their instinct and their hearts. The discerning recognize the dignity of his masterpieces. The indifferent dismiss him, «Utrillo is no longer in fashion. Enough of his postcards.» All the while, speculators make handsome profits on sales of his work.

His period of genius lasted a brief eight years. From 1906 to 1914, his paintings were pure inspiration. Those canvases rank him among the greatest landscape painters of the early twentieth century and he will always be part of the grand tradition of French art. For another ten years after 1914, his work is occasionally equal to his early efforts. Then, when alcoholism had taken its toll, he lost all trace of his former brilliance. Art historians insist on dividing artists' work into periods. For Utrillo, they have chosen five: Impressionist, from 1903 to 1907; «Impasto,» from 1907 to 1911; «White,» from 1912 to 1914; «Architectural,» from 1915 to 1919; and «Colorful,» in 1920.

The division is highly arbitrary. It is difficult to define the renowned «White Period» because it appears in stages before it bursts into bloom. After 1930, only hints remain. His style is transformed. His genius gradually ebbs until his death at the age of seventy-two in 1955.

To rediscover Utrillo, to vindicate him, seems an impossible task! I would nonetheless like to set the record straight, separate the wheat from the chaff, defend what is exceptional in his art, and clear the air of prejudice, enigmas, paradoxes, and contradictions, especially those that proliferated as his work declined.

Utrillo's home life and his social and artistic milieu can be pieced together from Alphonse Tabarant's biography published in 1926, the interviews by Georges Coquiot and Francis Carco, the incomplete memoirs of his stepfather, André Utter, that have been preserved at the National Museum of Modern Art in Paris (thanks to the bequest of Robert Le Masle, a friend of Suzanne Valadon), and from the «Autobiography of Maurice Utrillo, Landscape Painter.»

Utrillo wrote this autobiography from October 13, 1914, to January 16, 1918, while at the home of César Gay, a wine merchant who took Utrillo into his home at 1 Rue Paul Féval during World War I. I have consulted the manuscript, a large, cardboard-covered tome that the dealer Paul Pétridès found at an auction. Tiret-Bognet, a Montmartre painter, illustrated the text. The watercolors and their sometimes humorous captions depict an artist at odds with society.

Maurice Utrillo was thirty-one when he wrote the first page in his childish handwriting. His regularly shaped, sloping letters are traced meticulously onto lined paper, now yellowed

autobiographie
de
Maurice Utrillo
peintre-paysagiste.
illustrée par Tiret-Bognet.

« Butte Pinson » at Montmagny, 1905
Oil on cardboard, 17⅜″ × 16⅞″ (44 × 42.8 cm). Private collection

with age. A penciled line marks the margin. Capital letters are notable for their fine flourishes. By 1915, the strokes relax and overflow the line, the words dance incoherently «influenced by turns of fortune,» as the author explained. A calmer orthographer returns in the last pages. Clearly, lyrically, and with surprising powers of reflection and observation, and a sense of humor that is more painful than naive, he explains what seems most important to him. As in his painting, Utrillo abandons himself to spontaneous and direct expression of what he felt and what he lived.

One approaches Utrillo in stages. He was a secretive figure who, until his biography was found, revealed himself only in his paintings. His life revolved around his mother, Suzanne Valadon[1]. She was like a beacon. Her presence and her absences both dazzled and blinded him. Maurice lived in her shadow, pined for her when she was far from him, rejected her when she was close. He waxed lyrical about her when she hurt him, then maligned her. When that harm was done, he repented. He held her responsible for his smallest joy and his greatest pains.

This desperate love and deep hatred for his mother is clear from the prologue to his autobiography. Deliriously, he professed his faith: «From the depth of my soul, I bless and venerate this saintly woman as I would a goddess, a sublime creature of Goodness, Integrity, Charity, and Devotion, a woman who stands out from all others, a noble woman who raised me always to respect the strictest codes of Morals, Law, and Duty.

«Alas, I failed to follow her good counsel and let myself be dragged into vice. Imperceptibly, and by frequenting impure and lewd creatures, slimy sirens whose eyes embrace Perfidy, and I, a faded Rosebush, a repugnant drunkard, was transformed into an object of public Scorn and Ridicule.

«Alas, a hundred times alas... May the author of my days forgive me!»

This excessive, mad filial eulogy is hardly a fitting description of Valadon's tumultuous life. He exalted her, imagined her saintly when he was well aware she was not. He could not have her pure, so he destroyed her by destroying himself in the bistros of Montmartre. He chided himself for what he had become. He suffered, blamed himself, and drank to drive off the ghosts. He could not live within the confines of reality.

In «Torment of God,» Verdake, a painter of the Pont-Aven school, wrote in 1890 of Filiger, another mystic and miscreant, that artists like Utrillo «seek to compensate for the discord in their souls by creating art. They have no vitality to spare, so each work saps life from its creator. Aware of their waning vigor, they turn to alcohol, morphine or opium because the exalted state that drove them to create has left them bereft of life and spirit. They want to feel life once again, and to do so, they drink, scream, bluster, and rant... Only religion and God's help might drive them to self-revelation and to humility, give them prayer, and bring them strength, thus curing these pour souls.»

This infernal cycle—frustration in love, refuge first in alcohol then in artistic creation—began early in Utrillo's life. «Genius is nothing more than rediscovered childhood,» said Beaudelaire. As for Utrillo, he never grew up.

---

(1) Cf. Jeanine Warnod, « Suzanne Valadon, » New York: Crown, 1981.

Suzanne Valadon and Maurice Utrillo. Photograph

Handwritten page by Maurice Utrillo from «The Story of my Youth until Today»

THE SEARCH FOR A FATHER

Maurice Valadon was born on December 26, 1883, at one in the afternoon. He was the illegitimate son of Marie Valadon. It has never been determined beyond a doubt who the father was. His eighteen-year-old mother, herself born out of wedlock, was suddenly burdened with a family. An artist's model, she left home each morning to pose for celebrated painters such as Puvis de Chavannes, Renoir, and Toulouse-Lautrec. She did not always return home at night. Maurice's grandmother, Maman-Madeleine, a good Limousin peasant, was a hearty fifty-three. She was retiring, resigned, devoted, and impassive during eternal family disputes. Her daughter's portraits show her skin furrowed with deep wrinkles; her neck disappears into her shoulders and her expression is sorrowful, sometimes haggard.

What was to become of a child raised by these two women? Maurice's first cry came from 3 Rue Poteau one winter night. (Today the building houses « La Mandarine,» a fruit and vegetable shop, and there are few vestiges left of this area as described by Émile Zola and painted by Steinlen.) The story of his early years reads like the lyrics of a maudlin popular song. « Terrible Maria,» Degas' nickname for her (only later did she call herself Suzanne Valadon), went off to work each day and left Maurice with his grandmother. Maman-Madeleine had already raised four children and was not about to coddle the newcomer. His first portrait at the age of two drawn by Valadon shows a fine, lovely face, long blond hair, and a sweet and loving expression already in search of affection, tenderness, and protection.

The next home for the trio was 7 Rue de Tourlaque. Maurice was admired for his gentle good looks and his vitality, but his grandmother fretted over his excessive sensitivity

*Utrillo
as a Schoolboy
Photograph*

*Utrillo and his
Mother
Suzanne Valadon
Photograph*

« GUINGUETTE » AT MONTMAGNY, c. 1907
Oil on cardboard, 12⁹/₁₆″ × 20⁷/₁₆″ (32 × 52 cm)
Private collection

CHURCH AT VILLIERS-LE-BEL, 1909
Oil on canvas, 23⅝″ × 28¾″ (60 × 73 cm). Private collection

14

CHURCH OF
SAINT-MÉDARD, PARIS
c. 1908–09
Oil on canvas
32¼″ × 18¼″
(82 × 46.4 cm)
Private collection

15

« Petit Château » at Saint-Ouen, 1910
Oil on canvas, 23⅝″ × 31½″ (60 × 81 cm). Private collection

16

Paintshop at Saint-Ouen, 1909
Oil on canvas, 21¼″ × 28¾″ (54 × 73 cm). Private collection

and nervousness, « He is quite adorable, but I wonder what runs through his veins. At times he frightens me. » She remarked on his wild, almost fierce character and worried that he never laughed and did not like to play, much less mix, with boys his own age. Maman-Madeleine felt it useless to talk about the boy to Valadon, engrossed as she was in her love affairs and art.

A photograph of Maurice as a schoolboy is revealing. Well dressed in a black smock, a cape and a wide scarf, a cap and boots with laces, his satchel slung across his back, he grasps a stick he used as a cane. Materially he lacked nothing. But his diaphanous face, with its strange, private expression, betrays profound inner sadness.[1]

He was docile, conscientious, studious, but uncommunicative. He cowered and his cowering provoked bullies into beating him. Soon his angelic air gave way to his repressed passions, anger, capriciousness, and violence. At home he would smash everything he could lay his hands on and tore his exercise books to shreds. What caused these outbursts? Was it his mother's absences from home? Or was he lashing out at what he saw and heard?

Toulouse-Lautrec rented the third floor studio in the building where Utrillo spent his early years. Valadon often climbed the stairs to the studio where she was both the artist's model and mistress. No doubt the child observed the comings and goings of his mother, overheard the arguments between the two tormented artists, suffered through their separations and reconciliations. Jealousy and frustration must have intensified his sadness and the feeling he had been abandoned.

Valadon had suffered too much from being born out of wedlock to let her son remain without a name for long and she tenaciously set out to find a father for him. At one point she faked a suicide in an attempt to trick Toulouse-Lautrec into marrying her. Did the child perceive the ruse when his mother confided to Maman-Madeleine, « He would not go along, so I played my trump card »? Did Maurice see Toulouse-Lautrec's face when the artist discovered the ploy? Utrillo probably understood his mother's desperation over the burden of his illegitimacy and it must have made him feel guilty. He hated her for that. At the same time the shared torment brought them closer together.

Which of Valadon's many lovers in early 1883 could have been the real father? Maurice Boissy, a regular at the cabaret « Le Lapin Agile, » had the same first name. Tabarant peddles this idea in his books. Puvis de Chavannes often painted Valadon's portrait and he was Utter's candidate. But Puvis de Chavannes's nephew denied that the author of the *Bois Sacré* could be Utrillo's father. Or was it after all Miquel Utrillo, journalist and painter, who gallantly acknowledged the boy in 1891?

The brief idyll shared by the young Catalonian and the model ended when Miquel Utrillo returned to Spain. But in 1888 they met again in Montmartre and lived together for a few tumultuous months, arguing constantly.

When Maurice was eight years old, Miquel Utrillo, troubled by doubts over the boy's paternity, generously offered to give the boy his name. After being assured that the boy would not lose his French citizenship, he went to the town hall on the Rue Drouot and, in the presence of two witnesses, a clerk and a waiter, signed the necessary papers:

---

(1) See page 12.

18

Utrillo as a Child. Photograph

FACTORY AT SAINT-DENIS, 1910
Oil on canvas, 21¼″ × 29¾″ (54 × 75.5 cm)
Museum Bridgestone, Tokyo

20

«On this day, January 27, 1891, I hereby recognize as my son Maurice, born December 26, 1883, whose birth was recorded on December 29 at the town hall of the 18ᵗʰ Arrondissement as the son of Marie Valadon and an unknown father.

«Drawn up by Charles Paul Auguste Bernard, deputy mayor... on the declaration by Miquel Utrillo, 28, journalist, residing at 57 Boulevard de Clichy, who recognizes as his son Maurice...»

In March 1893, the Spaniard and the Montmartre model left each other for good. Erik Satie, the bohemian musician, and Paul Mousis, a well-to-do manager for the firm of Bel et Sanbéant, became Valadon's lovers. Mousis was to provide her with comfort and security for many years.

From then on Valadon and Miquel never mentioned their liaison. Valadon confessed that she herself did not know who Maurice's father was and the discreet Spaniard cut short all conversation on the matter. Today, Miquel's son, who lives in Sitgès and claims he is Maurice Utrillo's half brother, continues to try to establish his father's paternity of Maurice, but his evidence — several photographs showing a strong, even impressive likeness between the boy and Miquel Utrillo, and Miquel's letters that mention Valadon and Maurice — seem merely circumstantial.

THE LITTLE BOY IN THE WHITE BERET

At the age of eight, Maurice had a father whom he would never see again and a protector, Paul Mousis, who provided for the boy's education. A photograph shows Maurice snuggled in the arms of his very beautiful mother. Valadon sits precariously in a small corner of an armchair; Maurice seems to be pushing against her to be as near as possible and at the same time to take up as much of the seat as he can. His hand is in hers, his face is pinched, serious, and watchful. Clearly he is fearful that this privileged moment might be snatched from him.[1]

When he sat for her emotional drawings of him, Maurice existed for her alone. He was content to serve as her model, to savor this direct contact. The experience was a balm and a consolation.

Then, abruptly, Mousis changed the boy's daily routine. He had a comfortable middle-class home built in Pierrefitte, in the suburbs north of Paris. Instead of the three small, crowded rooms of the Rue Tourlaque, the family now had a spacious house in the country. In the new setting, Maurice would meet the children of the market gardeners, boys who were even cheekier than those of Montmartre. Utrillo wrote of his arrival:

«A young, rather elegant young woman accompanied by a venerable matron stepped down from the moving van. With them was a young, well-dressed boy wearing a pretty white beret.

_____

(1) See page 10.

CHURCH OF SAINT-GERVAIS, PARIS, 1910
Oil on cardboard, 21¼″ × 28¾″
(54 × 73 cm)
Private collection

RUE LEPIC, c. 1909–10
Oil on canvas, 28⅜″ × 23¼″
(72 × 59 cm)
Private collection

23

« I was that young boy and that childish headdress marked me as a city boy, a Parisian to boot, and gave me the reputation of being a swaggerer.

« One night, dressed as usual in my white beret, as I was running errands, I came across a young farmer who eyed me from head to foot. My appearance threw him into fits of laughter... »

To help Maurice adapt to his new surroundings, Mousis enrolled him in the Pluminard boarding school, « a splendid building with a large vegetable garden, a vast orchard and lawn, a huge playing field, and only mediocre tuition. »

The teachers were helpful with the new boy, but the bullies could not abide the « sissy. » They nicknamed him « Lagourde » (the blockhead). Maurice took revenge by drawing a merciless caricature of the band's leader, who quickly informed on the artist. Maurice was punished and thereafter contrived, unsuccessfully, to be one of the boys.

Maurice complained of his unhappiness and loneliness in a letter to his father. Exaggerating, he wrote:

Pierrefitte, January 1, 1896

Dearest Michel,

I could not begin the New Year without telling you I still love you and think of you often. I hope that everything your heart desires is yours soon. I beg of you, I want to see you. Why don't you send us news of you more often? Why don't you think of me? You are my father. Why don't you come and see us? I'm so unhappy because mother always tells me you will never come back to us again and I'm crying as I write you this New Year's Day. I'm alone with grandmother. Cousin Marie no longer lives with us and today Maman went to Paris to work. Mother is quite unhappy and always sick, you wouldn't recognize her she's aged so much, it's grandmother who told me to write you. Monsieur Paul came to put me in a boarding school in Pierrefitte, and since we've lived here he hasn't come back, and it's been three months since we've seen anyone. I'm rather bored and quite sad and so is grandmother. I've wanted to write you for a long time, but Maman didn't want to give me your address because she said you didn't want to see me any more. But I begged her so this morning before she left for Paris she gave it to me but she didn't want to know that I was writing to you. Dearest Michel, I'm not writing because I want you to send me a New Year's gift. Anyway, I'm too big now and I don't care in the least for gifts, I only want one thing, that's to see you soon because it makes me sad

(Catherine Banlin-Lacroix points out in her thesis on Miquel Utrillo that this letter was mysteriously delivered to Miquel Utrillo's son the night of Maurice Utrillo's funeral in November 1955.)

STREET IN THE OUTSKIRTS OF PARIS, 1910
Oil, 19⅝″ × 28¾″ (50 × 73 cm)
Private collection

« Rue Norvins, » 1910
Oil on cardboard, 22⅞″ × 28⅜″ (54 × 72 cm). Kunsthaus Zurich

« RUE NORVINS, » 1910
Oil on cardboard, 22¾″ × 27¹⁵/₁₆″ (58 × 71 cm). Private collection

« Café de la Tourelle » on Rue Lamarck, 1911
Oil on canvas, 19½″ × 28¾″ (50 × 73 cm)
Private collection

not to see you. If you are angry with maman, grandmother tells me to tell you that the letter you write me you should address to her so that I at least can hear from you. Grandmother sends you a kiss and I love you with all my heart and hug you as hard as I can.

Your son who would very much like to visit you.

Grandmother is sending you a portrait of mother when she was twelve years old that she found among her papers. She wants you to see how much it looks like me. But because mother knows that grandmother found the portrait, send it back to us as soon as you have seen it so Mother does not notice that we sent it to you. I send you another kiss, Papa. Write me soon.

Maurice Utrillo

Here is the address:

Madeleine Valadon, 18, avenue de Saint-Denis
Pierrefitte (Seine)

In his letter, the boy put his father on a pedestal. No doubt Maman-Madeleine pressured the boy into writing. She could not forget that she, too, had been abandoned by the father of her child and she used Maurice to remind Miquel of Suzanne. By doing so she intensified the boy's suffering and made him all the more conscious of his loneliness and confusion.

That year, on August 5, Mousis married Valadon. They had been lovers for three years. He gave her a studio on 12 Rue Cortot, where she painted and was relatively happy, while her son remained a victim of his own sadness and isolation.

THE RELUCTANT APPRENTICE

At thirteen, Utrillo received his diploma from the Pluminard boarding school and enrolled in Rollin high school (today the Jacques Decour Lycée) and took the train to school each day. His second year was quite successful:

« I took first prize in French and math and ethics (I am ashamed to say I cheated on one of the last ethics exams) and thus I was able to take part in the Charlemagne festivities. Pleasant memory of a sumptuous feast with superb wines topped by bubbling champagne. Then I gradually let up and sank into sloth. In geometry, starting with the famous theorem of the square of the hypotenuse, I must admit I was almost nonchalant, the class dunce, if you will... »

Utrillo fell to playing hookey. Wandering along the roads that led from the train station, he found adults who taught him to drink. With the pocket money supplied by

Mousis, he lured his classmates to the « Café des Oiseaux » on the Avenue Trudaine, where the welcome was warmer than that at his well-appointed suburban home.

Rather than repeat the third form, he left school in 1899 and at the age of sixteen set out to learn about life. His path was strewn with disappointments. For three months he was an errand boy for an English traveling salesman. Then, on the recommendation of Paul Mousis, he was hired by a bank, the Crédit Lyonnais, as a clerk and spent his time copying and adding columns of figures. He held that job until one day he broke his umbrella over a colleague's head. Utrillo believed the man had crushed his beloved bowler hat. In all his jobs he did his best to get himself fired as if to prove to himself that he was of no use to anyone.

There were innumerable other jobs from which he was ignominiously dismissed. Mousis wearied of coming to his rescue and refused to help Utrillo further. Left to his own devices, he became sullen, bitter. At Saturday dances in Butte-Pinson, he would provoke peasant boys into fighting with him and come home bruised and bloody.

With the complaints of her neighbors ringing in her ears, Valadon brought her son back to Paris and the Rue Cortot. But there he taunted the street urchins and they responded by beating him mercilessly. Life still seemed hopeless.

At eighteen he was treated for alcoholism at Sainte-Anne Hospital. Doctor Ettlinger, a friend of the family, advised Valadon to « help the poor boy from harming himself. Find him an outlet for his nervous energy. Why don't you teach him to paint? »

« Painting is what women like mother do, » thought Utrillo. Being told « Go paint, » to him meant, « Leave us alone, go dabble with your palette. » He had neither faith nor conviction in his own talent and had no intention of pursuing painting. He resisted but to avoid being excluded from the family circle, he daubed a few canvases with five colors chosen by his mother. Impressionist painting was at its height and instinctively his first work reflected the trend.

At first he angrily dragged his painting gear to the Montmagny apple orchards. No one was particularly interested in his dabblings. He filled his time as best he could until the day Valadon noticed one of his landscapes and told him, « You are doing quite painterly work. You just need to learn to draw. » She set herself the task of teaching him. He sulked. He found it more natural to paint the canvas directly without the discipline of a preliminary sketch. Valadon, on the other hand, had first learned to draw. Once she had mastered technique, she broke the rules and then took up oils. Forced to draw the shadow of a potato, her son flew into a rage, threw the sketch out the window, and tore up his sketch pad. It was a gesture he was to repeat whenever anyone tried to instill discipline in him.

Unfortunately, all of his drawings done in Montmagny in 1903 have disappeared.

Valadon often came to the Rue Cortot to work and sometimes brought her son. On one occasion, the painter Heuzé said of the shy, thin, almost skinny boy, « His face was long and bony, his gray-blue eyes glittered with gold, but there was something troubling in his eyes. A few hairs on his chin. His long hands were straight and distinguished and reminiscent of those painted by El Greco. They were the hands of a young girl and an aristocrat. »

Utrillo's first paintings are as innocent as his hands seemed: small, round trees scattered among orchards or lined up along roadsides, rows of tile-roofed houses against a wide, expansive sky. Calmed by the quiet and light of the countryside, he applied thick, generous strokes to the canvas.

ANGEL, DEVIL — AND GENIUS

Utrillo recalled these early days in his autobiography. « I began to paint about 1903 while in Pierrefitte and Montmagny. The first scenes were from Pierrefitte and the quais of the Seine in Paris. I did not leave my mother's side. I was told I was influenced by Pissarro. Perhaps there was a resemblance, but at the time there could not have been any influence. I had seen no paintings other than my mother's. But the despotism of painting is dictated by Chance and obeys "Neither God nor law." I followed my temperament as an artist, I painted as I pleased and I obeyed my inspiration that was dictated by my basically warm nature. »

From the fall of 1903 to the winter of the following year, Utrillo produced about one hundred and fifty canvases or sketches. In 1905 he signed *The Butte Pinson at Montmagny* [1] « Maurice Valadon; » others he signed « M. U. Valadon, » and from 1906, « Maurice Utrillo, V, » leaving a trace of his mother's name as if to legitimize his work. In his painting Utrillo thought he had found freedom; in truth, it was another form of maternal alienation.

Now Utrillo's work showed promise and Mousis was proud to show it to his employers who bought them for a pittance to decorate their offices.

Utrillo set up his easel in Paris, Montmartre, and the Quai Saint-Michel, [2] the suburbs close to Paris, Saint-Ouen, and Saint-Denis. It took him one session before his subject, working furiously and in an almost feverish frenzy, to produce a masterpiece.

Two personalities coexisted in Utrillo: the angel or mystic manifested itself in his work; the alcoholic dragged him into disgrace.

« I vegetated for a while in an infuriating inactivity incompatible with my nervous, bold nature. One day, when I could stand the boredom no longer, I had a monstrous or ingenious inspiration. I took my drawing pad, a few colors, and some kerosene (for lack of oil) and went to practice that difficult and ungrateful art known as painting in a typical Montmartre corner. Was this the root of my anguish caused by an ignorant riffraff? My beginnings were difficult. My efforts were greeted by stones and sarcasm from inebriated onlookers. I persevered nevertheless.

« When I myself believed what I painted was good, I mused, " It is Sisley, all right." Why Sisley, I shall never know. I had seen nothing of this master's work but I had heard mother talk of him. I repeated that name. How silly can you be at first? »

Utrillo was more restless than silly. He had no master and was full of self-doubt. He needed to be reassured, to have a yardstick, and Sisley was an established name. In his

---

(1) See page 8.   (2) See page 5.

memoirs, Utrillo often offered incisive, intelligent explanations of his work. «At times my paintings appear to be in relief. That is because I keep coming back to the same work. Only for the skies do I do my utmost to make them as clear and transparent as possible.»

Utrillo's skies alone reveal his genius. «His leaden, swollen, crushing skies, thick with air, seem to absorb the light rather than reflect it,» wrote Francis Carco. «How they hang heavy in his early work. Some are ghastly and conjure up death stalking in the early morning. Others, with their somber thickness, remind me of huge railway stations where steam rushes up to form immense floating mattresses of soot.»

SACRED INSPIRATION

Between the end of 1907 and the fall of 1910, Utrillo painted almost seven hundred landscapes devoid of people: small churches, cathedrals, walls covered with graffiti, dilapidated façades with or without windows. The *Rue Lepic*[1] and the *Petit Château of Saint-Ouen*[2] of 1910 are still impressive, while *Street in the Outskirts of Paris*[3] marks the beginning of the White Period.

The five-volume catalogue raisonné edited by Paul Pétridès, Utrillo's dealer from 1936, lists 2,489 paintings. In a few months Utrillo would use the same setting from the same angle several times, without, however, imitating the Impressionists, who captured the light at different hours. Contrary to appearances, these are not reiterations of the same paintings, but reflections of the painter's varying moods in a setting he would repeatedly return to. A church or a Montmartre street «shocked his senses» and moved him to paint. Thus the Clignancourt church,[4] on the Place Jules Joffrin near his birthplace, was the subject of ten of his canvases in just two years. «The church is not particularly beautiful or old,» he confided to Georges Coquiot, a critic, «and it just stands there alone. But I love it just the same and painted it for mother to keep.»

His emotions propelled him to transcend what he saw. He used the image before him as an anecdote, a pretext to support his lyricism and affectivity. This is precisely why it is impossible to link him to any artistic movement. Maurice Utrillo is neither naive nor self-taught. He is not a visionary like Rousseau, Séraphine or Bauchant.

He denied all outside influence, especially that of his mother, who never did wish to sway him. This is undoubtedly one of the reasons he painted rather than drew. His contrary nature preserved his personality and sheltered him from any temptation to become a «follower.» He was possessed by an obligation to express the shock to his senses.

On July 14, 1908, his *Notre-Dame with Flags*, vibrant and bathed in light, shimmers as if freshly bathed by a storm. It depicts a holiday. I can almost hear the bells peal, so much does this painting convey intense, inner joy. For a moment, the artist seemed freed of the guilt and sins that tormented him.

---

(1) See page 23.   (2) See page 16.   (3) See page 25.   (4) See page 66.

LIGHTHOUSE IN BRITTANY, c. 1911
Oil on canvas, 23⅝″ × 32″ (60 × 81.2 cm)
Private collection

STREET AT MONTMARTRE, 1911
Oil on cardboard, 19⅝″ × 29½″ (50 × 75 cm)
Private collection

34

THE HOUSE OF BERLIOZ, 1912
Oil on cardboard, 20⅝″ × 29⅝″ (52.5 × 75.5 cm)
Private collection

« IMPASSE COTTIN, » 1911. Oil on cardboard, 24³⁄₈″ × 18¹⁄₈″ (62 × 46 cm)
Musée National d'Art Moderne, Centre National d'Art et de Culture Georges Pompidou, Paris

The joyous cathedral signals the beginning of a sacred inspiration, a veritable path to glory in the artist's work: from *Notre-Dame* to the *Church at Villiers-le-Bel*[1], as robust and as indestructible as a fortress against an opaque sky. He was a tireless pilgrim, and through his paintings he was to journey to *Saint-Denis, Sainte-Marguerite, Saint-Médard*, the cathedrals of Chartres, Rheims, Moulins,[2] and so many others.

Heuzé bought the *Church of Deuil* for thirty francs and later renamed it the *Little Communicant*. «For me, this church is purity incarnate,» said Heuzé. «This extraordinary thing was in some ways a confession. The church is bordered by a small cemetery whose tiny door is painted green, the color of hope. The green seems to pardon the ivory of the tombstones and the despair of the mourners who come to pray for those buried there. It was not merely a masterpiece. It went beyond the limits of painting.»

More modest structures, such as the *Conquet* in Brittany, or the *Murato* in Corsica, *Montmartre, Saint-Ouen, Saint-Jean-au-Bois* or *Saint-Hilaire*[3] exalt the same symbolic image: a protecting goodness, a cavern much like a womb.

When they are wide and massive, his churches are shaped like cavernous wombs. The doors are closed, but a secret light might glow in the nave to dispel all baseness from the soul, rekindle warmth in bruised hearts, and reassure the lost and abandoned.

Utrillo swelled the volumes to make these miraculous houses of worship immense. Outside, the steeple points toward a sky gilded with rays from an invisible sun. This must be the celestial light of true believers and primitive painters. The concentration, the loftiness, the simplicity are spiritual. Certain canvases are reminiscent of Giotto, whose religion of the soul became a religion of the heart with more appeal to sensitivity than to intelligence.

«Utrillo doesn't invent, he transmits.» He gave what he received humbly and unconsciously. A universal light illuminates his work.

FIVE FRANCS FOR A MASTERPIECE

How did a painter whom few took seriously and most ridiculed become the prey of art dealers?

According to Tabarant, the frame maker Anzoli was the first to publicly display an Utrillo painting. In 1905, he hung in his shop on 4 Rue de la Vieuville, around the corner from the Place des Abbesses, a view of the Paris embankments that Valadon had exchanged for a frame. The canvas drew the attention of such connoisseurs as Degas, Mary Cassatt, and Signac, who noticed it as they left orders for the white, rounded frames made fashionable by Seurat, the creator of Neo-Impressionism.

Others sold Utrillo illicitly off the street. With one eye out for prospective buyers and the other for the police, a junk dealer (Sérat) and a butcher (Jacobi) sold daubs on the sidewalk in front of «L'Abbaye de Thélème,» a cabaret on the Place Pigalle. Occasionally they would have a recent painting by Utrillo to hawk to passersby. Tabarant purchased

---

(1) See page 14.   (2) See pages 47, 15 and 78.   (3) See pages 54, 43 and 41.

his first Utrillo, a view of the Eiffel Tower, from one of these would-be dealers for about ten francs.

Prices increased steeply when Clovis Sagot got wind there might be money to be made with Utrillo. For the ridiculous sum of three francs he bought a few sketches and exhibited them next to Picasso's *Pink Mountebanks* in his Rue Lafitte Gallery.

«Sagot was a sly old fox who had no scruples and knew no pity,» Fernande Olivier, Picasso's campanion at the Bateau-Lavoir, used to say. «He set up his gallery in a former pharmacy, where he came upon some old stocks of medicine, which he then generously offered to ailing artists. But he was canny enough to recognize the potential worth of a beginner...»

Utrillo's scenes of Montmartre went on sale at Sagot's for between five and ten francs. Sagot sent others to Switzerland, where they fetched up to fifteen francs. In Munich, the *Rue de la Barre* and *The Steps of the Sacré-Cœur* hung next to works by Cézanne, Van Gogh, the Fauves, and the Cubists. Yet there were few buyers.

«You've certainly got talent,» Sagot told Utrillo, «but you are influenced by Sisley and Pissarro. Shake them off, for God's sake. Do not drink yourself to death and put your nose to the grindstone. If you are willing to work, you can wallow in money.»

Libaude was another art lover with a keen eye. At Sagot's he noticed Utrillo's 1909 *Notre-Dame de Paris* and the artist's original technique of incorporating plaster into paint. The asking price was eighty francs, but Libaude wanted it for less. He immediately contacted Valadon and offered her fifty francs. He wrote her, «The price shall remain our secret. I hardly ever buy the work of young painters any more but I will make an exception in the case of your son because I find his talent particularly interesting...» The deal was made. Libaude had negotiated a thirty-franc discount on a masterpiece.

Louis Libaude was a curious figure. Francis Jourdain noted his mournful expression and his frail health and likened him to a «cardsharp at a funeral.»

Libaude worked as an auctioneer and writer (his pen name was Louis Lourmel). He was the author of «Tableaux d'Ame» and the founder of the magazine «Rénovation Esthétique» that Emile Bernard laid out in his studio at 12 Rue Cortot. When Libaude came across paintings that might bring in a profit, he temporarily set aside work on such books as «Pensées d'un Solitaire,» «Cœur Volant,» «La Grande Famille,» a patriotic novel, and «L'Ecuyère,» a one-act play. He was to play a key role in Utrillo's future.

One rainy day, while leaving Sagot's gallery, where he had failed to sell his landscapes, Utrillo showed a passerby his work. The stranger was none other than Pissarro's son, who quickly promised to find him a buyer.

The next day, at five in the morning, Utrillo called at the Manzana-Pissarro home. «He staggered in, bumped into a piece of furniture, lost his balance, and managed to get his head wedged behind a trunk. My wife and I had a devil of a time pulling him out. He had brought us about thirty paintings!»

Manzana contacted Libaude, yet another coincidence, one that proved to be quite a windfall for the dealer. With a fine set of Utrillo's work that he had gradually put together with purchases from junk dealers, Libaude attracted the art critics to his gallery on the Avenue Trudaine. Francis Jourdain brought Elie Faure, Octave Mirbeau, Paul Gallimard, and the Kapferer brothers. Each one of them bought paintings by this unknown artist whose work was « reminiscent of Pissarro's finest period. » The praise in their columns finally drew attention to Utrillo.

A PAINTING FOR A DRINK

Still, Utrillo had to scrounge to buy a drink. He tried to sell his paintings as he finished them. At the opening of another artist's show at Druet's Gallery on the Rue Royale, Utrillo arrived with a selection of his own work. The public was amused but only the gallery's accountant bought anything — the *Trees in Bloom at Montmagny*, for forty francs.

Druet was a former café owner and could not abide drunkards. He ran Utrillo out of the gallery. Ever tenacious, Utrillo set up a makeshift exhibit in the vaulted archway leading to the gallery and peddled his work for less than five francs apiece. An old photograph captures him in his bowler hat seated on a stool surrounded by his landscapes. He had posted a sign that read: « Exhibition and Sale of Paintings. » In his own hand he added, « ... By Maurice Utrillo, daily from 2 to 7 p.m. at Gay's, 1 Rue Paul Féval, 18ème. »

Roland Dorgelès remembered that « he shouted, " For five francs, less than you'd pay inside." Because he was dressed in rags and sold for next to nothing, no one would buy. » He was constantly snubbed, yet he never gave up hope.

In 1909 he was invited to exhibit for the first time at the Salon d'Automne, but his entry, *The Bridge of Notre-Dame*, went practically unnoticed. At the same time Dorival, an actor at the Comédie Française and a collector, bought three paintings, *The Moulin de la Galette*, *The House of Berlioz*,[1] and *Rue Norvins*, directly from the artist.

Utrillo's willingness to sell directly to collectors disturbed Libaude, who was anxious to ensure his exclusive rights to Utrillo's work. Much like a school principal who wanted to talk to the mother of a brilliant student, Libaude summoned Valadon to a meeting. After much exaggerated politeness on both sides, he concluded a contract for Utrillo's entire production in exchange for a modest monthly retainer to be handed directly to Valadon.

The next day, Utrillo arrived at Libaude's with his mother. He was cleaned up, dressed decently, and made a good impression. The contract was signed. But the partnership led to bitter arguments. Utrillo would throw fits, beg for money, refuse to speak, and sneak out — the classical behavior of an alcoholic deprived of drink. To live up to the contract, Valadon had to hide the paintings so that Utrillo could not spirit them out of the house to barter them for drink.

Libaude proved to be as stingy, exacting, and unrelenting as a blackmailer in a story by Eugène Sue or Victor Hugo. The mother could be as temperamental as the son and both could and did revile Libaude mercilessly. Although terrorized by the infernal duo, the dealer became increasingly tyrannical. For example, on the pretext that his clients disliked Utrillo's elaborate signature, he obliged Valadon to sign her son's work in a small, fine hand and insisted that the painter limit his production. Exasperated, Utrillo offered his paintings to another dealer, Marseille, on the Rue de Seine. For her part, Valadon threatened to reveal Libaude's

---

(1) See page 35.

ridiculously low retainer. In the end, she gave in to the dealer's demands. She needed the money to pay for her son's mounting medical bills.

Utrillo was now completely dependent on alcohol and desperate to know, «Does anyone love me?» This question sums up his life's torment. He painted to deaden his sense of loneliness and express his feelings. But was there anyone willing to accept them? Who understood him? He found no one in his desperate search. Gradually he became more deeply entrenched in his tragic isolation.

Utrillo wrote, «For the indiscriminating, all artists are creatures with long hair, baroque ideas, and eccentric life styles. We are bizarre extraterrestrials, outlaws. The bourgeoisie — merchants, workers, civil servants, and others — shuns the artist, except when it wants to bathe in the glow of art or obtain our work at a better price... How disillusioning and how malevolent and prosaic the Montmartrois are.»

His love frustrated, he took refuge in drink. His «grind,» as he often called his work, safeguarded and delivered him from his fear of others. His art exorcised his demons, kept him from the «evil ones,» the «horrid,» names he used for those who snubbed, beat, and exploited him.

He was made light of, manipulated, and left defenseless, like Dostoevski's «Idiot.» He had nothing left but to paint, his only means of communication with the world and the only way to prove himself to himself. Society rejected him as it does poets whose truths are unbearable. «It's lousy,» cried the neighborhood shrews, but they, at least, took pity on the forlorn, woozy artist. Others threw stones at him. Pity and malice, both reactions are the due of the artist who dares show the public disturbing work, a new truth. He was persecuted and treated like a simpleton, a village idiot. But he knew he was not, and never had been, out of his mind.

«I have never been mad,» he told Carco. «It is just that my drinking leads to uncontrollable outbursts. If I were crazy would I paint like I do?»

His wrinkled jacket, skinny legs, and floppy wide pants gave him the appearance of a vanquished Don Quixote, his dream ripe for snatching. He bartered his paintings for innumerable glasses of wine, and the paintings disappeared into bistro cupboards and the hands of shrewd dealers. Humiliated, he said, «One should rank artists or award them stripes to wear on their sleeves so that everyone could easily judge their worth. I would be a sergeant, I suppose.»

The more fervently he sought love, the more aggressive he became and the harder the blows fell. Francis Carco, André Warnod, André Salmon, Pierre Mac Orlan, and others saw him as a martyr.

Carco wrote, «The Montmartre hill was his daily torment and the bistros so many stations of the Cross where the rabble reviled him as he carried out his mission. All the elements of the Passion were assembled: the jeers of the crowd, the beatings by the police, and the desperation of his mother. On those nights God had truly abandoned him.

— Who knows the cross I bear, asked Utrillo?
— I know your burden, replied his friend Heuzé. Ailments of the heart and soul can rarely be cured.»

CHURCH AT SAINT-HILAIRE, 1911
Oil on cardboard, 19¾″ × 25⅝″ (50 × 65 cm)
The Tate Gallery, London

Rocks at Ouessant, 1912
Oil on canvas, 23⅝″ × 31½″ (60 × 81 cm)
Musée National d'Art Moderne, Centre National d'Art
et de Culture Georges Pompidou, Paris

42

43

STREET AT STAINS, 1910
Oil on cardboard, 19¾″ × 29⅛″ (49.5 × 73.5 cm)
Private collection, New York

44

Once, after a row between his mother and Mousis, who reproached Suzanne, «You make less of a fuss when your son comes home drunk out of his mind than when he distorts a perspective.» Utrillo was able to express his anguish. «Mother's husband loses his patience more often than ever. One day she will have to choose between him and her drunkard of a son and she won't be able to make the choice,» he wrote. His abyss grew deeper and wider.

His mental health, already quite fragile, was now to receive perhaps its greatest shock. In 1909, Valadon took Utter, one of Maurice's friends and two years his junior, as a lover. She married Utter on September 1, 1914.

The boys had met for the first time in 1906. Utter was looking for a subject to paint in the Montmagny countryside and saw a strange figure crouched in a field. It was Utrillo at work on a canvas. The two returned to the house together where Utter met Valadon. For Maurice, it was the beginning of a friendship. For Valadon and Utter, it was love at first sight. Three years after that chance meeting in the field the «unholy trinity,» as the critic Robert Beachboard called it, moved, for better or for worse, into 12 Rue Cortot.

THE WHITE PERIOD

The year 1912 was a good year for the painter. He produced a masterpiece a day. Two of these were the *Rue Norvins*[1], whose leaden and green sky reflects on the white walls of humble houses while in the distance rises the milky, uncanny dome of the Sacré-Cœur, and the *Factory at Saint-Denis*[2] with its poignant sadness. The fine, light bricks of the factory chimneys stand against a stormy sky; the water in the canals seems as thick as that in a cesspool. One small glimmer of hope: a ray of sun hits the pink wall of a humble suburban house.

His inspiration alternated between hope and despair. The *Rue Sainte-Eleuthère*, with its high, narrow, shutterless windows and its symphony of black and white, and the *Rue de Crimée* are more austere than the *Church of Saint-Gervais*,[3] which looms over the banks of the Seine lined with ochre houses whose blue roofs announce inner joy on a sunny winter day.

The first still lifes appeared in this period: a few bouquets of flowers, a blue jug done in a slightly awkward style. «To tell the truth, I have never done a still life,» he said. «Yet fruits and flowers, inanimate objects, are not disquieting. Yes, I believe that, but without realizing it, I am far too impressed by the first inanimate object that catches my eye, that I want to retain my attention. You know, you get an idea, you see forms easily. That's why I don't like to remain alone with a cat. All at once, a cat will begin to chase something invisible in the air and immediately I feel ill at ease.»

In numerous paintings, he meticulously inscribed words taken from walls. The names of wines, liquors, messages of love, hearts pierced with arrows. He wryly wrote on the fence of the «Moulin de la Galette,» «Artistic painting factory. Specialists in landscapes. Fine Colors. Maurice Utrillo, V, 12 Rue Cortot. Paris 18. Beware of forgeries.» Humor, misery, and loneliness were all he had. All the while he yearned for affection.

---

(1) See pages 26 and 27.   (2) See page 20.   (3) See page 22.

STREET, c. 1917
Oil on canvas, 18″ × 21⅝″
(46 × 55 cm)
Private collection

CHURCH OF SAINTE-MARGUERITE, 1910–12
Oil on cardboard, 28⅜″ × 19⅝″
(72 × 50 cm)
Private collection
▷

THE VICIOUS CYCLE

Utrillo got drunk on wine, rum, eau de Cologne, denatured alcohol, and benzene. After a bout of delirium tremens in June 1912, he had to be admitted to an asylum. Valadon and Utter were forced to ask Libaude for the money to cover his treatment. Tabarant described the melodramatic scene:

«Libaude placed a table between himself and his visitors and clutched a small bell. He then screeched, "The meeting is in session." As Suzanne Valadon began to speak, she was interrupted by the jangling of the bell. "Your son has the floor, Madame!" dictated Libaude. Utrillo remained silent... and when Utter tried to get in a word, the jangling became frenetic.»

Valadon was finally able to explain that her son urgently needed to be placed in an asylum and there was no money to pay for his care. Then Libaude furiously rang his bell and thundered that her request constituted unbearable pressure on him. «I shall not give in! I will not be a party to it,» he repeated. Again Valadon tried to speak, but he paid her no heed and gave the bell a final ring, «The meeting is adjourned.»

A few days later Libaude, afraid of losing the goose that laid the golden egg, relented and agreed to deposit three hundred francs per month to the account of Doctor Revertégat in Sannois to cover Utrillo's room and board. In exchange he demanded a fixed number of paintings.

Utrillo seemed almost delighted with his retreat and wrote: «The staff treats me well, the food is excellent. There is nothing but purified water to drink, the room is quite comfortable and there are all sorts of things to do to keep one busy. Smoking and coffee are permitted after lunch and at 4 p.m.» There, far from his daily torments, his art could mature.

But in the *Avenue Rozé* at Sannois his desire to flee is apparent. A fine wire-mesh fence all but hides the hospital in the background. This 1912 canvas, with its light and transparent colors, its lightheartedness, expresses deliverance, a maturity and self-assurance no one ever dreamed him capable of. There were also bouts of depression. The twisted tree that he painted behind an iron gate suffers as he did in the asylum. Verlaine[*] wrote, «Endlessly runs the lane underneath the fine and paling sky,» as if referring to this painting of Utrillo's with its obsession with glimpsed but unattainable freedom. Ever alone — no one listened to him — he talked to himself for days on end.

The treatment was a success and his mother and stepfather accompanied him to Brittany to visit their friend Chaudois, a chemist, from Montmartre. Utter wrote, «The trip to Ouessant was epic. The dogs came along. It was a circus. How were we supposed to work under such conditions?»

Utrillo was left with a painful memory of the visit to, «as the chroniclers called it, "this earth of dread and land of the shipwrecked." Sorrow, nostalgia rather, pervaded my entire being.» The deserted heath, the scraggy meadows, the barren rocks of Ouessant,

---

(*) « A Nest for Lovers, » from « Romances sans Paroles. » Translated by Brian Hill. In Paul Verlaine, « The Sky Above the Roof, » New York: Collier Books, 1962.

Church at Fère-en-Tardenois, c. 1912. Oil on canvas, 31½″ × 23⅝″ (81 × 60 cm)
Musée d'Art Moderne de la Ville de Paris

and the lighthouse at Creac'h, [1] echoed his sullen and taciturn nature. The paintings he brought back were as desolate as the countryside; nothing grew there but lichens. Utrillo had one fervent wish: to return to Montmartre. « I secretly and ceaselessly longed for the Ile de France, the City of Lights, movement, the vicious yet familiar circle where all human passions, hateful and beautiful, intermingle. »

Back in Montmartre, he turned to prostitutes, « those creatures of pleasure who lead him to commit acts that took renewed energy and courage to recover from, » who terrified him and left him full of guilt.

In *The Arrest* he depicts the police taking him to the station house on the Rue Lambert. This descent into the inferno was relieved by a few happy moments with Marie Vizier, whose cabaret « A la Belle Gabrielle » was on the Rue du Mont-Cenis. « Across the way I lived the happiest moments of my life. Maurice Utrillo, October 1920, » reads the signature on one of his paintings. An arrow indicates that the inscription is meant for Marie Vizier, who is pictured on the doorstep. The buxom blond was a great source of kindness, yet she, too, wronged him and beat him mercilessly. César Gay, the former policeman and owner of the « Casse-Croûte, » generously took him in at night when he was driven out of the Rue Cortot for creating a public disturbance.

He could count on help from Adèle at the « Lapin Agile, » on the Rue Norvins, near the « Bateau-Lavoir, » where Picasso's little band lunched. Adèle was always good for a free meal in exchange for a painting.

Utrillo's first important exhibit was organized by Libaude in Eugène Blot's gallery on the Rue Richepanse. From May 26 to June 9, 1913, Blot showed thirty-one paintings executed in 1912 and 1913: the *Church of Montmagny*, landscapes of *Sannois* [2], *Saint-Leu Taverny*, the *Saint-Aignan Church at Chartres*, *Chapel at Roscoff*, and numerous views of Paris, especially Montmartre. He was at the peak of his White Period. He had completely changed his palette, widened his strokes, and applied the white paint with a knife. To make the whites even whiter and reinforce the symbol of purity, he mixed in plaster and glue to render his walls more lifelike (*The Debray Farm at Montmartre* [3]).

Plaster fascinated him. Francis Carco once asked him what he would carry away with him from Paris. He replied, « A few of those fragments of plaster to touch and gaze at and that enable one to think. »

« I got it into my head that only plaster, real plaster, could give me the marvelous effects I wanted. And it fell apart, it cracked too quickly. I so longed for the truth that I wanted to paste real objects, grass, leaves, on my paintings... »

Despite Libaude's flattering preface to the catalogue, the critics gave the exhibition at Blot's short shrift and the public largely ignored it. Fame was still a long way off. Two paintings sold for seven hundred francs. The dealer was furious, but Utrillo was bored to distraction by the business of selling and left for Corsica with his mother and stepfather.

In Corsica each of the three painted the sky, mountains, and the stone houses in his own fashion. The setting was a complete contrast to Montmartre. Utrillo was dazzled by the sun and freed of the thick walls that oppressed him. He created his most beautiful

---

(1) See pages 42 and 33.   (2) See pages 52 and 53.   (3) See pages 64 and 65.

masterpieces. *The Church and Parish House at Murato* conveys primitive innocence. Its small trees scattered over the hillside are bathed in a golden light covered by a peaceful, biblical sky. The light of the *Street in Corte* is harsher; the red roofs sing in the peaceful stillness. His painting became light, serene, spiritual. It was a moment suspended in time just before the war.

MONSIEUR MAURICE

Despite his patriotic fervor, Utrillo was unfit for military service and he spent the war in Montmartre. Maman-Madeleine died in 1915 and Valadon joined a wounded Utter in the Lyons region, leaving Maurice in the care of César Gay. A now wiser boarder said, «There, at least, no rakes or revellers could get at me.» He used the time well to write his «Mémoires.»

The Montmartrois had dropped his nickname «Maumau» and now addressed him as «Monsieur Maurice.» He had climbed a step up the social ladder. Francis Carco, a poet and a kindred soul, was all too familiar with the painter's agony and better than others knew how to get close to Utrillo. He first wrote of him in 1921:

«The first time I laid eyes on Utrillo he was not in the street, disheveled and staggering. I met him one winter's night on the Montmartre hill at Monsieur Gay's, who was looking after Utrillo and keeping him from lapsing into his dissolute wanderings.

«The room contained a bed, a chair, a mirror, and an easel and overlooked the steps of the Rue du Mont-Cenis. A bare lamp with no shade cast a sickly light on the walls...

«He had put down his pencil and ruler and a shy smile, mocking yet resigned, froze on his face like a painful twitch. That smile! I shall never forget it. It looked like a ghastly mask with two little ellipses for eyes that let the light shine through to reveal the sweet, tender, almost childish gaze of a child or a recluse. The gaze was contradicted by the grin on his lips that betrayed his bitterness. There was too much constraint in it to be a smile; it was too mechanical, had too much maniacal rigidity, sly embarrassment, too much deceptiveness.

«Looking at him, I was surprised how closely he resembled the idea I had come to have of him from his painting. He had an aura that was exalted yet troubled and pained. He seemed submissive and hostile to himself, mistrustful and artless, confusedly sensitive and cunning...»

César Gay advised Carco, «Do not be embarrassed to call him Monsieur Maurice. It reminds him of his childhood... If I wanted to see him leave, I would only have to call him Utrillo... The name alone drives him to drink.»

In his small room Utrillo took his inspiration from landscapes on postcards (for example, *Rue Saint-Rustique*[1]). With a compass, a try square, a plumb line, and a ruler,

---

(1) See page 70.

STREET AT SANNOIS, c. 1912–13
Oil on canvas, 23⅝″ × 31½″ (60 × 80 cm). Private collection

STREET AT SANNOIS, c. 1913–14
Oil on canvas, 23⅝″ × 31½″ (60 × 80 cm). Private collection

CHURCH AT MURATO, CORSICA, 1913
Oil on canvas, $23^{5}/_{8}'' \times 31^{1}/_{2}''$ (60 $\times$ 80 cm)
Private collection

54

« Le Lapin Agile, » c. 1913
Oil on canvas, 23⅝″ × 31⅞″ (60 × 81 cm)
Private collection

« Rue Tholozé, » 1913
Oil on cardboard, 22⅜″ × 30⅝″ (57 × 78 cm)
Private collection

he knew that his houses would be well crafted. « With those gadgets I am sure not to make a mistake.» Then he would remember the scenes he had gazed upon for hours as he sat dejected in front of the doors that had been closed on him. He had spent entire nights roaming the streets. The shutters of the Rue Tholozé, the signboards of the Rue Lamarck, the bars of a gate, the slopes of a canal, the reflections of the street lamps glistening with rain, and the hundred steps of the *Impasse Cottin* [1] that were so difficult for him to climb — all these were imprinted on his memory forever. These fleeting visions nourished his work.

Utrillo explained to Coquiot, « You see a cathedral and the houses around it. For the moment, I shall apply generous strokes of color. I will raise the walls, I will be the mason, then the carpenter, the roofer. Only when its basic supporting color is in place will I fill in the details. I love them, those immense, high walls, white or gray, or yellow, or red, or pink. They need their doors and windows. Roofs need to be covered with zinc or tiles. With shutters each slit has to be counted. You cannot imagine how useful all these details are.»

A PICTURE POSTCARD

Images paraded before him like frames from a bad film in which he was playing the lead. What did it matter that he painted from picture postcards; he added his truth to the images. Nonetheless, the method disturbed him. Was he not cheating nature? Would he lose the « essential emotional shock » and, as he told Carco, « reject the impression for itself and return to the canvas not the impression but only the object? »

His devotees had never had much respect for him. When they learned that « Maumau » was using postcards, he fell further in their esteem. They accused him of enlarging photos, of turning out fakes, and not caring for anyone's opinion. No one, however, tried to understand the wretched painter.

This reputation dogged him until the thirties, when the United States Customs Service blocked about twenty of his paintings that were shipped for an exhibition at the Valentine Gallery in New York. Customs argued that the paintings were picture postcards and not paintings. Art critics, museums, even Utrillo himself, were outraged. But they lost the case. According to the law, original oil paintings are exempt from customs duty, but to take the paintings out of customs, the gallery had to pay a supplementary tax.

Helpless without his mother, Utrillo once again made the rounds of the asylums and hospitals: Villejuif, Aulnay-sous-Bois... On August 1, 1917, he wrote Valadon, « Your place is in the Louvre and mine is in a mental home. I realize I threw my life away when I was sixteen and it's now too late for me to fit into bourgeois society. I am sensual, intelligent enough, and hardheaded.

« Ask for my support and I will be more than a son to you; I will be your slave. But a demon torments me — alcohol.»

---

(1) See page 36.

In his drunken stupor, he translated news from the front of bombings, fires, death and destruction into views of French villages laid waste by accursed enemies in pointed helmets.[1] In *Rheims Burning* his anger roared with the flames that licked the stones of the ornate Gothic cathedral. Rheims was not just another church to him, but a «Titanesque work of beauty» whose soul was left mortally wounded. Under his brush, the cathedral trembled and suffered. The destruction of the holy place where Joan of Arc crowned her king was a sacrilege Utrillo could not endure. A mystic, he venerated Saint Joan. She was his spiritual mother. Like a child who needed to be reassured by a beloved object, he wore her effigy day and night.

During the four years of World War I, Utrillo painted about twelve hundred canvases. At least two hundred of them are masterpieces. Once again at Villejuif among the insane, he saw the world in colors. Translated onto canvas, the work expresses a rage to live. The cracks in his walls have disappeared. Strident green leaves now cover the walls. Churches glow red. His paintings compensated for the sun he could not possess and filled his longing to give and to triumph over evil.

Four months out of Villejuif and he was once again roaming the streets, resting only when someone would take him in — César Gay, Delloue, the junk dealer on the Rue de Clignancourt, and all the cheap wine dealers who stored his paint boxes. Bistro owners covered their walls with paintings by Monsieur Maurice. In Montmartre everyone, even

(1) See page 68.

*Utrillo in his Studio
on Rue Cortot
Photograph*
◁

▷
*Utrillo, Suzanne Valadon
and Utter
in the Studio on
Rue Cortot
Photograph*

the police, knew that the slightest scribbling by Utrillo was worth something. His prices broke records in auctions, starting on May 2, 1914, with the sale at «La Peau de l'Ours,» when four sketches — *Notre-Dame de Paris, Landscape at Montmagny, Village Street*, and *The Square* — hung with works from Picasso's Blue Period, to March 24 and 28, 1919, at the sales of the collections of Octave Mirbeau, the writer, and Eugène Descave, a former police officer.

«It is a story unparalleled in the history of art,» wrote André Warnod. «Without any desire on his part, a painter had attracted countless disciples who neither liked nor admired their master. With his rise to fame, Utrillo was sought out by hordes of unqualified dealers and unscrupulous daubsters.»

Hundreds of forgeries flooded the market. He was plagiarized, imitated. The forgeries and the copies sold for ludicrously high prices. Yet buyers snapped them up as fast as they could be turned out. They were content to find anything signed «Maurice Utrillo, V.» They hoped one day to trade their oils for a solid gold bar. The frenzy stopped only when

Georges Coquiot and Utrillo. Photograph

buyers realized it was better to make inquiries first rather than fall into a forger's trap later.

While his paintings were being traded like blue-chip stocks, Utrillo followed events from afar. In 1919, he slumped into a deep depression and was hospitalized in the Picpus Asylum among the violently insane.

Zborowski, Soutine's dealer, took over from Libaude. For five or six paintings a month, he paid Utrillo's room and board at the asylum. To defray the medical expenses, he had to turn to collectors, Jones Netter, the industrialist, and Levasseur, the propeller magnate.

A MEETING IN MONTPARNASSE

Meanwhile, the patient was being persecuted by his warders, who also had taken to stealing his paintings. He escaped and headed for Montparnasse, where he was less well known than in Montmartre. He soon met Modigliani, his brother in misery and a fellow slave to Bacchus. Their mutual admiration became legend. According to Francis Carco, the two contracted with Mère Rosalie to decorate the walls of her restaurant on Rue Campagne-Première, where starving artists could always count on a meal. One portrayed a Montmartre street and the other put in the figures. Rosalie did not like their painting and sent them packing. The two alcoholics made their exit arguing, « You are the greatest painter, » Modigliani told his companion. « No, you are the best, » protested the other. Their nocturnal carousing attracted the attention of the police and Utrillo once again found himself in the Picpus Asylum. He remained there from July 11 to August 24, 1920, according to the asylum's bills.

Modigliani and Utrillo were to meet very different destinies. Modigliani died poor at the age of thirty-five. He never knew glory and left behind an exemplary body of work. Utrillo died at the age of seventy-one, doted upon in a comfortable suburban house in Le Vésinet. Shut up in his religion, he painted canvases devoid of love and remained unaware of the art dealers' transactions concerning his work.

As Utrillo withdrew into his private darkness, his painting turned precise to the point of dryness. His old streets and churches lost their pure, primitive quality and became almost too technically perfect. What was once an emotional realism turned into a set of crude tones in which each house had its careful details but lacked soul. It was as if Utrillo, victim of his own vice and no longer capable of projecting himself into his paintings, left behind only meticulously drawn outlines and vivid colors, such as *Sacré-Cœur with Flags*[1], from his Architectural (also called Cloisonné) Period.

Some called them sterile, others believed them magic. According to Carco, there was something tragic in this new style. He saw them « deliberately stripped of their eloquence, but slyly harboring a secret. »

HOUSE ARREST

As was almost inevitable for an alcoholic, Utrillo was arrested and charged with lewd and lascivious behavior. At the Santé, he had two pickpockets for cellmates. He wrote to César Gay: « Inform my family that I have been threatened with six days in solitary confinement for drawing on the walls. »

The press outcry mobilized public opinion and the public prosecutor had Utrillo transferred to the Sainte-Anne Hospital. But caring for the artist became increasingly difficult. Valadon and Utter already had power of attorney over Utrillo's affairs. Now they had to give their word that they would take responsibility for him at home.

Utter wrote to the police commissioner:

« This is to inform you that after a meeting on July 31, 1921, at the mental ward of Sainte-Anne... my wife and I hereby swear that as soon as M. Maurice Utrillo is released we will undertake full responsibility for his care. We will keep him under constant surveillance at our home on 12 Rue Cortot, where he will have a room of his own.

« We also agree that if he shows the slightest inclination to drink, we will see to it that he is returned to an asylum. We are fully aware of the task we are undertaking and we assume full responsibility for it. »

Utter then warned Utrillo, « I have written to the police commissioner and formally agreed to engage a nurse to care for you at home so that you might be released from the asylum and returned to your family. You must understand that I can neither let you drink

---

(1) See page 73.

nor offer you the means to obtain drink, for example, give you your paintings or money. If you wish to sell a painting to one buyer rather than another, write to that person and have him come to the house. Together we will buy whatever you need. My commitment prevents me from allowing you to come and go as you wish, as you must be accompanied at all times. Home or the asylum, the choice is yours. There it is, straight out. André Utter, May 27, 1921. Paris, 12 Rue Cortot.»

And Utrillo signed, «Read and approved.»

Commitments and promise brought little change in Utrillo's routine. Confined to his small room on the Rue Cortot and watched over by a nurse, he played with his toy trains or spent hours dejected and resigned at the window. Suddenly he would throw his paints and brushes through the bars and listen to the clatter they made as they fell to the pavement. They could leave, they could be free. Each outburst was followed by a period of calm. He painted from picture postcards and scribbled his poems on slips of paper, on the back of drawing pads, or in notebooks.

«I lampoon injustice, slander; my tender poetry extols virtue, innocence,» he told Coquiot. «I like Gothic literature, tales of adventure, and Dumas' cloak-and-dagger novels. To me, Victor Hugo makes for the best reading, but there are too many volumes for a painter who works every day. I like philosophical writings. Goethe wanted to express his concept of nature and man in symbols. I take pleasure in that since man hardly interests me, at least not to paint him.»

Stays in nursing homes now became milestones in his life. He alternated between treatments for alcoholism and sojourns in the country. In 1922, Valadon and Utter accompanied him to Brittany to visit Georges Aubry, a collector and friend. Valadon's liaison with Aubry sparked numerous arguments and outbursts of jealousy, and the trio soon departed. Utrillo bitterly regretted being forced to leave «yet another house where I shall never be welcome.» It was a profound disappointment for this forlorn character who so desperately longed for just one place where he might feel at home.

«CHÂTEAU LA POMPE» BEAUJOLAIS

Other trials awaited him at Saint-Bernard, near Villefranche-sur-Saône, where in 1923 Utter bought a crumbling château, thinking that the clean country air would do the entire family good.

Money was no object from the moment Valadon signed a contract with the dealer Bernheim. Utrillo shared in the abundance. In late June 1924, he pulled up to the château in a sumptuous Panhard driven by a liveried chauffeur. His head was bandaged; he was recovering from head injuries inflicted when he banged his head against the wall out of fear that he was to be sent to an insane asylum after being picked up by the police. For a time his family feared for his life. But his feeble mien belied a strong body and he recovered quickly and again picked up his brushes.

Castle of Saint-Bernard, c. 1925.   Postcard

The Debray Farm at Montmartre, 1924.   Lithograph

THE DEBRAY FARM, c. 1914. Oil on canvas, 28³⁄₈″ × 24³⁄₄″ (72 × 63 cm). Private collection

« Notre-Dame de Clignancourt, » c. 1913
Oil on canvas, 23″ × 30⅛″ (58.5 × 76.5 cm). Private collection

THE HOUSE OF MIMI PINSON AT MONTMARTRE, 1913
Oil on canvas, 22″ × 29½″ (56 × 75 cm). Private collection

House after Shelling, c. 1915
Oil on canvas, 22¾″ × 30⅝″ (58 × 78 cm)
Galerie Koller, Zurich

Landscapes at Anse [1] marked his « recovery, » but his palette was no longer so sober. Whites had made room for harsh blues.

At « Château la Pompe » (the « House of Adam's Ale ») as Utrillo called it, wine was prohibited and Eden became Hell. He disturbed the people playing bowls and insulted bigoted churchgoing women. But the inhabitants of Saint-Bernard would not put up with this rich and famous Parisian.

In a fortress reminiscent of a set for Hamlet, « Maurice could yell and scream as much as he liked. Suzanne could answer him in kind. Only the ramparts and the fish in the Saône could hear them, » recalled Utter. Whenever Utrillo's outrageous behavior provoked anger, he threatened to throw himself into the river or terrorized the gatekeeper, a kind woman from the village, by kicking down her door in the middle of the night.

He spent his days dreaming of Montmartre. In the Beaujolais hills, he painted Paris bistros and the « Moulin de la Galette. » He repeated the same themes to please his public, but he had lost the creative force of his earlier years. He painted dozens of *Lapin Agile* and *Rue du Mont-Cenis*, all without his earlier verve.

Utrillo's colors bewildered his old clientele and the dealers hounded him to continue his White Period. « This is sheer slavery! » he confided to Francis Carco. « All they want is white, but that is not the half of it. There is green and red. What idiots! »

Carco found the colored work every bit as miraculous as the white canvases and defended Utrillo vigorously before all critics. Nevertheless, treatments for alcoholism alternating with drunken sprees were taking their toll. The contrasts were harsh, the skies lost their ether, the paint no longer had its rich thickness, and was applied now without transitions to fill in the volumes. But some of his magic remained. He was still a master of technique and he occasionally managed to create extraordinary work, but his soul was no longer in his painting.

Utrillo seldom painted portraits. There was one of a clown and another of a *Japanese Man* he met in Montmartre, done in a style not found elsewhere in his work. About 1916, he painted Madame Zborowska, wife of the dealer for Soutine and Modigliani, who had come to his rescue on several occasions. But he felt incapable of painting a self-portrait.

Why did he refuse to paint himself or those close to him? Utrillo explained to Coquiot, « I believe I am too shy. I cannot look people straight in the eye, so I cannot paint them well. Sometimes I do paint human figures, but the farther in the background they are the better I like them. As for women, I give them more prominence, but I hardly follow fashion. Their big buttocks and hips must make you laugh. I see them all as mother hens. Mother paints her women with big buttocks, and I must have been influenced by her. »

Tabarant found another explanation for these « wenches... They are womanly. They exude a violent, peppery, spicy sexiness evocative of the dances on the Butte Pinson or the Montmartre alleys that reeked of urine, the slopes of the fortifications, the vaults where the sour odor of wine mingles with the smell of mussels and fried potatoes. The ladies with large buttocks embody sexual obsession. »

---

(1) See page 77.

« Rue Saint-Rustique » at
Montmartre, c. 1916
Oil on canvas, 21⅝″ × 18⅛″
(55 × 46 cm)
Private collection
◁

« Place du Tertre » and
« Sacré-Cœur » of Montmartre, c. 1916
Oil on cardboard, 20⅞″ × 29½″
(53 × 75 cm)
Private collection

71

At first glance I think that these figures seem like immovable, decorative pawns. Pissarro reduced his passersby to small colored dots that blended into his composition. Utrillo treated them like statuettes in his landscape. (See the *Restaurant de l'Étang des Ecrevisses at Chaville*, [1] 1923, and *Place du Tertre at Montmartre*, [2] 1925.)

He drifted out of the present and took refuge in his memory. Kiki de Montparnasse remembered: « I posed for him and then looked to see what he had done. I was astounded to see that he had drawn a small country house. » He no longer used postcards, but drew from his accumulated store of images. He copied what his memory conjured up, but he no longer created, and what he considered « unusual » was merely banal, insignificant, and barren. The flame flickered, but enough mastery remained to bewitch his collectors and keep his prices up.

In the twenties, record-breaking figures tell the story: the price of his paintings, the number of paintings, exhibitions and auctions, reviews and buyers. The very abundance dazed Utrillo: contracts, a château, a town house, a car with chauffeur, the Legion of Honor. Yet he lived threatened with prison if he drank anything stronger than water.

The year 1925 was prosperous and glamorous. The Hodebert-Barbazange Gallery showed sixty works from 1910 to 1914 and confirmed Utrillo's genius. As indifferent as ever to public enthusiasm, he scrutinized his work at the show, rubbed his hands together, and left the gallery without a word.

On February 17, 1925, he was officially declared incompetent and all remaining legal authority over him and his affairs — sales of paintings, payment of debts, purchase of furniture and property — was transferred to his mother and stepfather.

THE TREASURE CHEST

On the Rue Cortot, Suzanne Valadon was besieged by collectors. They knew the best paintings were hidden in a wardrobe and they all wanted a « wardrobe Utrillo. » But the keeper of the treasure would only unlock the door for emergencies or for close friends. Carco was one. He rediscovered the *Church at Fère en Tardenois* [3] and others that Utrillo had offered him for ten francs and that Bernheim bought for a fortune as part of their contract from 1927 to 1929.

Finally a *Street at Montmartre* was included in the 1925 exhibition, « Fifty Years of French Painting, » at the Pavillon de Marsan and Utrillo took his rightful place in the history of French art. Utrillo did not bother to attend the event. He continued to paint from behind the bars of his window.

In the issue of « Art Vivant » of March 1, 1925, Edmond Jaloux extravagantly compared Utrillo to Dostoevski's Prince Myshkin and declared that Utrillo had done for Paris what Canaletto had done for Venice, Vermeer for Delft, Piranesi for Rome, and Whistler for London:

---

(1) See page 82.   (2) See page 83.   (3) See page 49.

« SACRÉ-CŒUR » WITH FLAGS, 1919. Oil on canvas, 31½″ × 23⅝″ (81 × 60 cm). Private collection

THE POLICE STATION AT VILLEJUIF, c. 1915–17
Oil on cardboard, 20$^{1}/_{16}$″ × 29½″ (51 × 75 cm)
Private collection

74

« Till my Last Horse, I Said, » 1917
Oil on cardboard, 18½″ × 23⅝″ (47 × 60 cm)
Private collection

VIEW OF ANSE. THE CHURCH AND THE SURROUNDINGS OF SAINT-ROMAN, 1925
Oil on canvas, 25½″ × 31⅝″ (65 × 81 cm)
Musée National d'Art Moderne, Centre National d'Art et
de Culture, Georges Pompidou, Paris

Maurice Utrillo, V,
Juillet 1922,

78

CATHEDRAL AT MOULINS, 1922
Oil on canvas, 47½″ × 30⅜″
(122 × 77 cm)
Private collection
◁

CHURCH IN THE LOIRET, 1921
Oil on canvas, 17¾″ × 23⅝″
(45 × 60 cm)
Private collection

« Moulin de la Galette, » 1922
Gouache, 7⅞″ × 10¼″ (20 × 26 cm)
Private collection

« Montmartre Cancans »
Satirical Poem, 1927

« L'Etang des Écrevisses, » a Restaurant at Chaville, 1923
Oil on canvas, 18⅜″ × 21⅜″ (47.7 × 54.5 cm)
Private collection

MAURICE UTRILLO Paris, 1 p.m., 26 December 1883

Utrillo's horoscope is marked by a great ambivalence, with the following main aspects:

(1) Strong dominance of planets in earth signs (Capricorn, Taurus, Virgo), giving his paintings a profound sense of the concrete. Neptune in Taurus and in the Ascendant explains the inspiration, mysticism and light in his work and also his tendency to alcoholism.

(2) Sun square Uranus: a person of genius and hence poorly understood, who uses his art to convey his inner drama. The Moon, Lord of the Fourth House, opposed to the conjunction of Saturn and Pluto; exaggerated attraction to his mother and problem posed by the absence of his father. Feeling of frustration, stress, conflict and inner anguish periodically pushing him to the limit of a mental instability exacerbated by alcoholism. All his lucidity is preserved by the Capricornian influence.

Diagrammatically, Utrillo's work is marked by the double signature of Saturn and Neptune. Saturn: architecture; Neptune: mysticism. (Frequency of churches in his paintings.)

* * *

It is the dynamism of Utrillo's horoscope that explains his development and hence the different periods of his artistic career:

IMPRESSIONIST PERIOD (20–25)

Important aspects of the progressed Moon, Uranus and Saturn in transit:
— The progressed Moon, Lord of the Fourth House, is transiting natal Uranus (genius).
— Uranus is passing the square of natal Uranus and the trine of natal Jupiter.
— Saturn is transiting all the planets in the Tenth House (social achievement), is in the trine of natal Uranus, and then the square of natal Neptune.

It is thus the « meeting » of the Moon (his mother), Uranus (genius) and Saturn (practical realization). This leads to the artistic awakening of the horoscope, owing to the predominant role of his mother (Moon), which helps to reveal his own genius (Uranus). This is the beginning of his existence in society (Tenth House) and of the practical realization (Saturn) of his aspirations (Uranus and Neptune).

IMPASTO PERIOD (25–28)

— Pluto (matter) is passing to the square of natal Uranus.
— The progressed Moon is transiting the natal Moon.

These two aspects coincide with the use of matter on canvases (Pluto) and with the appearance of persons (Moon).

WHITE PERIOD (29–31)

— Neptune (light) is in the sextile of natal Uranus.
— The progressed Moon is in the trine of natal Neptune.

A symbol of perfect purity, Neptune dominates this period, nurtures his genius (Uranus) and becomes attuned to his sensitivity (Moon).

ARCHITECTURAL PERIOD (32–36)

Important aspects of Saturn in the Fifth House (creation): in conjunction with natal Jupiter and Mars and with the square of natal Neptune and Saturn. Need to accentuate qualities of stringency and structure (Saturn).

COLORED PERIOD (37)

Two aspects are dominant: Saturn, Lord of the Tenth House, is transiting Uranus, is trine of these planets in the Tenth House (success, honors). The conjunction of Jupiter and Neptune is transiting the Fifth House. These aspects, which are not contested by others, are certain to bring honors, success and recognition of his artistry. The color and presence of women also appear in his paintings.

Horoscope by J. GRUAU

HOROSCOPE

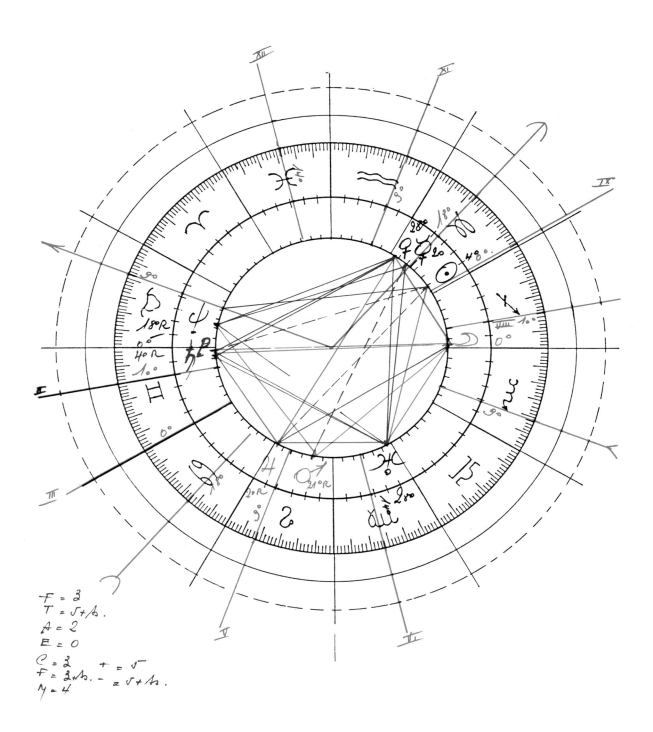

«I have seen him work at dusk in his little room at the vast canvas that was to become one of the most important views of his cherished " Moulin de la Galette." He could hardly see, but the semidarkness seemed to revive his spirit. The canvas was covered with a geometrical design traced with minute attention to detail and almost exaggerated precision. It was the drawing of a schoolboy — a schoolboy of genius.»

In June 1925, a sketchbook published by E. Frapier appeared with four lithographs in black and white dated 1924: *Notre-Dame de Paris*, the *Place du Tertre*, *The Debray Farm at Montmartre*, and the *Cabaret du Lapin Agile*. He later etched the *Moulin de la Galette* and the *Rue d'Orchampt*.[1] Vlaminck had convinced him to work on stone; he had gone to some pains to do so, for drawing had always been quite difficult for Utrillo.

The same year, the Bernheims purchased a house under construction for him. It was on the Avenue Junot in the shadow of the sails of the Moulin de la Galette.

The «Unholy Three» moved in January 1926. At Number Eleven, wrote Tabarant, was a row of small houses reminiscent of tiny cottages, jammed together and closed off by wooden gates. Utrillo's was the last on the left. Entering, there was a corridor, the kitchen, dining room, and a vast studio at the lower level where Utter worked. On the second floor, to the left, were two small rooms. One contained Utrillo's wrought iron bed, the other was his studio/cell. There he gathered his few mementoes and his child-man playthings. Suzanne Valadon had her studio in the small garden.

Life had already been difficult in the Rue Cortot, but it became unbearable in the new house. Although money was no object, the threesome argued incessantly. Utter wrote Valadon, «Wishing to be neither witness nor author, nor victim of a tragedy, I must flee this atrociously sick man and this disastrous atmosphere...» Utrillo returned to Sainte-Anne on July 6, 1926.

The 1925—35 Depression had little impact on the painter. Another event, however, his baptism in Lyons, on June 8, 1933, when he was fifty years old, was more important: it brought some peace to his troubled soul.

Valadon had constantly worried over the fate of her son. When in 1935 she underwent surgery at the American Hospital in Neuilly, she conceived the idea of marrying him to Lucie Pauwels, widow of a Belgian banker, a friend of the family, and an artist who signed her work «Lucie Valore.» Up to now all attempts to find a wife for Utrillo had failed. It took two years for Valadon to see her idea put into practice.

THE DOORS TO THE NIGHT

How many times has the scene of Utrillo leaving his mother been described? The descriptions are usually pathetic and burlesque. The truth is simple and moving. After numerous arguments between Valadon and Utter over Maurice, separation was inevitable.

(1) See pages 86 and 87.

« Notre-Dame, » Paris
1924
Lithograph

« Rue d'Orchampt »
1925
Lithograph

87

THE HOUSE OF MIMI PINSON AT MONTMARTRE, 1940
Oil on cardboard, 21⅝″ × 27¹⁵/₁₆″ (55 × 71 cm)
Private collection

Maurice Utrillo followed Lucie out the door proclaiming, «And now, long live liberty!» He was fifty-four; Lucie was sixty-six.

The marriage was celebrated on April 23, 1937, in Paris, and later in Angoulême, where Lucie Valore owned some land and a house, «La Doulce France.» The marriage was blessed at the Saint-Austone church by Monsignor Palmer, chaplain to the Spanish royal family. «Thanks be to God, I am married,» said Utrillo.

The couple soon returned to Paris and set up house in Le Vésinet, in the former home of Antoine Bourdelle. Utrillo was looked after by his wife-mother who for twenty years saw to his every comfort. He prayed in his private chapel and painted his views of Montmartre, now little more than hollow images.

Francis Carco visited his old friend just before Utrillo's death. He cast an embarrassed glance at the canvases that lay strewn around the studio. No one was fooled. In spite of his condition, Utrillo seemed aware that his former genius had waned. «Oh, I work, you know. I never stop. Get it?» This familiar expression conjured memories of friendship between the two men. Both of them were moved to find each other again.

Carco noticed a life-size photograph of Suzanne Valadon, dressed in a white smock, palette in hand.

«It's splendid always to have her here before me, next to me,» said Utrillo, rubbing his hands together as he had in 1925 when he found his masterpieces on show at the Hodebert Gallery. Then he murmured: «I am never alone, never. Even when I pray,» he said, pointing to an authentic thirteenth-century altar set on top of a chest of drawers, «I can see her.»

— «Do you pray for her?»
— «Yes,» he answered, blowing a kiss toward his beloved image.

* * *

On November 5, 1955, Maurice Utrillo died of pulmonary congestion at the hospital in Dax.

His funeral was held on November 9 in Montmartre's Saint-Pierre chapel, which he had so often painted, and he was buried in the small Saint-Vincent cemetery next to the Lapin Agile that figures in so many of his canvases. On his last walk through his «village,» Utrillo was accompanied by hundreds, both friends and strangers. A light rain fell.

BIOGRAPHY

1883 Born the illegitimate son of Marie Clémentine Valadon (Suzanne Valadon) at one in the afternoon on December 26 at 13 Rue du Poteau in Paris. Birth recorded on December 29 at the registrar of the 18th Arrondissement. In January of that year, Valadon had met Miquel Utrillo, a painter and journalist, and Paul Mousis. The former officially recognized the boy eight years later; Valadon married Mousis in 1896.

1886 He lives with his mother and maternal grandmother, Maman-Madeleine, at 7 Rue Tourlaque, where Toulouse-Lautrec rents a studio.

1891 Miquel Utrillo formally recognizes Maurice at the registrar of the 9th Arrondissement.

1893 He leaves Montmartre with Maman-Madeleine for the Paris suburb of Pierrefitte. Valadon and Mousis commute between Pierrefitte and Montmartre, where Suzanne has a studio at 12 Rue Cortot.

1896 Valadon marries Mousis on August 5.

1897 Maurice leaves his private school in Pierrefitte. In the autumn, he enrolls at the Rollin school.

1898 He is awarded second prize in mathematics and an honorable mention in French.

1899 He even wins a mention for ethics. Nevertheless, he has to leave the Rollin school, as he is already an alcoholic and teachers consider him unfit to pursue his studies. On recommendation of Mousis, he becomes an apprentice in several banks and business firms, but never stays there for long.

1901 He abandons the search for work, indulges in heavy drinking, and wanders around the Pierrefitte-Montmagny countryside. He is forced to undergo his first treatment for alcoholism at Sainte-Anne Hospital.

1903 A physician, Dr Ettlinger, advises Valadon to interest her son in painting. Between 1903 and 1904 Maurice paints one hundred and fifty canvases. His early pictures of Montmagny resemble Impressionist paintings of the day. His early drawings are lost. He paints Montmartre, Paris, and the suburbs.
Mousis builds a comfortable house at Butte Pinson, near Montmagny, on the Route de Groslay. Maurice commutes between Butte Pinson and the Rue Cortot. Tutored by Quizet and Heuzé, he paints in the open air.

1905 Utrillo sells his first paintings to Anzoli, a framer, and to some junk dealers.

1907–10 Period of the heavily impasted streets and cathedrals. This is not the « White Period, » which did not start until 1911, when Utrillo mixed plaster and glue with his paints. First auction sale of his paintings.

1909 Utrillo exhibits for the first time at the Salon d'Automne.
Valadon leaves Paul Mousis for André Utter, also a painter. The three artists and Maman-Madeleine move to the Impasse Guelma in Paris, then to 12 Rue Cortot.

1910 Signs contract with Louis Libaude. Paints first still life.

1912 He is discovered by Francis Jourdain and Octave Mirbeau. Exhibits for the first time at the Salon des Indépendants. Show in Munich.
In June and July, he is treated for alcoholism by Dr Revertégat in a Sannois hospital.
Visits Brittany with his mother and Utter.
Georges Coquiot discovers Utrillo's work and introduces it to art lovers.

1913 Libaude organizes the first important Utrillo exhibition at the Eugène Blot Gallery, Rue Richepanse, from May 26 to June 9.
Utrillo is again treated for alcoholism at Sannois. Visits Corsica.
He lives at times with Marie Vizier at «La Belle Gabrielle,» Rue du Mont-Cenis in Montmartre, and with César Gay, keeper of the « Casse-Croûte, » Rue Paul Féval. This is the height of his « White Period. » He signs a contract with a new dealer, Marseille, Rue de Seine.

1914 Suzanne Valadon marries Utter, who then leaves for the war. Utrillo is turned down for military service. He stays with César Gay and on November 21 starts writing his autobiography. Auction at « La Peau de l'Ours » on May 2, where Level buys four sketches.

1915 Maman-Madeleine dies.

1916 From August to November, he is confined in the Villejuif asylum for the mentally ill. He paints exclusively from postcards. Zborowski, a dealer for Modigliani and Soutine, begins to sell Utrillo's work.

1917 He exhibits with Valadon and Utter at the Bernheim-Jeune Gallery.
In June Valadon joins Utter, who has been wounded in the war, in Belleville-sur-Saône.
Utrillo lives with César Gay.
In October, first article on Utrillo by Francis Carco in « Carnet des Artistes. »
Utrillo lives at times in the junk shop owned by Delloue on the Rue Clignancourt and in a hotel on the Rue des Poissonniers.

1918 From March 1 to August, he is treated for alcoholism in a hospital at Aulnay-sous-Bois. There he paints seventy landscapes to pay the medical fees.
March 9, auction sale at the Hôtel Drouot of the Libaude Collection.
In September, Utrillo goes to live with César Gay. On November 19, he signs a contract with Delloue. He then gives fifty paintings to Delloue as a settlement to terminate the contract.
Voluntarily enters Picpus Asylum. Zborowski pays for the treatment there.
He escapes from the asylum and meets Modigliani.

1919 On February 19, the Octave Mirbeau Collection is sold at the Durand-Ruel Gallery (*The Pink House, Rue de l'Abreuvoir,* which Libaude had sold for 150 francs in 1910, sells for 1,000 francs).
On March 28, the Eugène Descaves Collection is sold. *Notre-Dame de Paris,* painted in 1912, fetches 1,580 francs.
Critics begin to mention Utrillo in the press. In the spring, he is again committed to the Picpus Asylum for the mentally ill for one year.
Zborowski calls on two collectors, Netter and Levasseur, to help pay the monthly bill of 720 francs. In exchange, the collectors are given five or six paintings.
In December, Utrillo exhibits forty-six paintings, done between 1910 and 1915, at the Lepoutre Gallery.

1920 On May 19, six paintings belonging to Libaude are sold on auction at the Hôtel Drouot. *The Rue du Mont-Cenis* fetches 2,700 francs. The dealer had bought the six paintings between 1912 and 1914 for 200 francs.
On June 9, the Zamaron sale. *The Church at Villiers-le-Bel* is sold for 3,800 francs.

1921 He is arrested for lewd and lascivious behavior. At the Santé prison, he is threatened with six days' solitary confinement for drawing on the walls. He is transferred to the Sainte-Anne Hospital and later to a mental home at Ivry.
Exhibits at Berthe Weill's. First women « with large buttocks. » Article by Francis Carco in the « Nouvelle Revue Française. »

1922 In April and in October, he exhibits at Berthe Weill's together with Valadon. Exhibits *The Cathedral at Moulins* at the Salon d'Automne. Shows thirty-five paintings that formerly belonged to Marie Vizier, at the Paul Guillaume Gallery.

1923 Shows at the « Salon de la Folle Enchère. » Utrillo/Valadon shows at Berthe Weill's and at Bernheim-Jeune's.
Utter buys a crumbling castle in Saint-Bernard, on the banks of the River Saône.
First lithographs.

1924 Show at the Bernheim-Jeune Gallery.
After a spell in Ivry asylum, he spends the summer in Saint-Bernard.

1925 Participates in the show « Fifty Years of French Painting » at the Pavillon de Marsan. Shows at the Fiquet and Barbazange galleries.
A book of his lithographs is published by E. Frapier.

1926 He designs sets and costumes for the Serge Diaghilev ballet « Barabao. »
The Bernheims have a house built for Utrillo at 11 Avenue Junot. Mother and son move into the new house in January. Utter continues to live on Rue Cortot.
Biography by Tabarant is published.

1927 He signs a contract with the Bernheims.
Visits Saint-Bernard in October.

1928 He is awarded the Legion of Honor. The ceremony is held at Saint-Bernard.

1929 The contract with the Bernheims is not renewed. Utrillo meets Paul Pétridès for the first time.

1932 Exhibition at the Moos Gallery in Geneva.

1933 He is baptized in Lyons on June 8.

1935 On April 18 he marries Lucie Pauwels, also known as Lucie Valore, at the town hall of the 18th Arrondissement. She is the widow of Robert Pauwels, a Belgian banker. Religious ceremony in Angoulême.

1936 He exhibits at the Pétridès Gallery in Paris, and at the Adam's Frères Gallery in London.
Moves to Le Vésinet.

1937 On January 1 he signs a one-year renewable contract with Pétridès. Subsequent contracts with Pétridès were signed every two years until Utrillo's death.
He exhibits at the Tate Gallery in London, in Glasgow, and at the Bignou Gallery in New York.

1938 Suzanne Valadon dies on April 7. Utrillo does not attend the funeral. He spends days praying in his private chapel.
Exhibition at the Pétridès Gallery.

1939 Exhibition at the Valentine Gallery in New York.
He visits Le Lavandou.

1942 Exhibitions at the Albright-Knox Art Gallery in Buffalo (New York) and the Kunsthalle in Basel.

1947 The Pétridès Gallery holds an Utrillo retrospective with works from 1905 to 1913.
Utrillo does twenty-two color lithographs for Francis Carco's « Montmartre Vécu. »

1948 He designs sets for Gustave Charpentier's opera, « Louise. »
André Utter dies.

1950 At the Venice Biennial, one room in the French exhibition hall is dedicated to Utrillo's work.

1955 He is commissioned to paint two panels to decorate the meeting hall of the Fine Arts Board, and ten lithographs for « Paris Capitale » by André Maurois.
On November 5, he dies of pneumonia at the hospital in Dax, with Lucie Valore and Pierre Benoit at his bedside.
On November 8, his body is returned to Paris and lies in state in the crypt of the Sacré-Cœur. Funeral is held next morning at the Church of Montmartre. He is buried at Saint-Vincent cemetery in Montmartre.

BIBLIOGRAPHY

APOLLINAIRE, Guillaume. *Chronique d'art 1912–1918.* Paris: Gallimard, 1960.

BANLIN-LACROIX, Catherine. *Miquel Utrillo i Morlius, critique d'art.* Paris: Université de Paris IV, October 1971.

BASLER, Adolphe. *Maurice Utrillo.* Paris: Crès, 1931.

    Lettre sur Maurice Utrillo. Paris: La Belle Edition, September 1924.

BEACHBOARD, Robert. *La Trinité maudite: Utter, Valadon, Utrillo.* Paris: Amiot-Dumont, 1952.

CARCO, Francis. *Maurice Utrillo, étude critique.* Paris: NRF, 1921.

    La Légende et la vie d'Utrillo. Paris: Grasset, 1928.

    De Montmartre au Quartier latin. Paris: Albin Michel, 1927. *The Last Bohemia: From Montmartre to the Quartier Latin.* New York: Henry Holt & Co., 1928.

CASO, Paul. *La Vie tragique d'Utrillo.* Paris, Brussels: G. M. Dutilleul, 1956.

CHAMPIGNEULLE, Bernard. *Utrillo.* Paris: Editions universitaires, 1959.

CHANSON, André. *Utrillo.* June 1930.

CHARENSOL, Georges. *Maurice Utrillo.* Paris: Chroniques du Jour, 1929.

CHARMET, Raymond. *Utrillo.* New York: French and European Publishers, 1963.

COQUIOT, Gustave. *Cubistes, Futuristes, Passéistes.* Paris: Ollendorf, 1921.

    Maurice Utrillo, V. Paris: Delpech, 1925.

    Les Peintres maudits. Paris: Delpech, 1924.

COUGHLAN, Robert. *The Wine of Genius. A Life of Maurice Utrillo.* New York: Harper & Brothers, 1950.

COURTHION, Pierre. *Utrillo.* Lausanne: Jean Marguerat, 1948.

    Utrillo et Montmartre. Geneva, Paris, New York: Skira, 1956.

CRESPELLE, Jean-Paul. *Montmartre vivant.* Paris: Hachette, 1964.

    Utrillo, la bohème et l'ivresse à Montmartre. Paris: Presses de la Cité, 1970.

Utrillo, églises. Paris: Hazan, 1956. *Utrillo, The Churches.* London: Methuen, 1960.

    La Vie quotidienne à Montmartre. Paris: Hachette, 1978.

DAUBERVILLE, Henry. *La Bataille de l'Impressionnisme.* Paris: Bernheim-Jeune, 1967.

DE POLNAY, Peter. *Enfant terrible: The Life and World of Maurice Utrillo* (rev. ed.). New York: William Morrow, 1969.

DORGELÈS, Roland. *Bouquet de Bohème.* Paris: Albin Michel, 1947.

    Quand j'étais montmartrois. Paris: Albin Michel, 1963.

    Préface. Paris: Galerie Charpentier, 1959.

DORIVAL, Bernard. *Les Etapes de la peinture française contemporaine.* Paris: NRF, 1946.

DOUGLAS, Charles. *Artist Quarter: Reminiscences of Montmartre and Montparnasse in the first two decades of the twentieth century.* London: Faber & Faber, 1941.

FELS, Florent. *Utrillo.* Paris: Librairie de France, 1927.

    Maurice Utrillo. Paris: Druet, 1930.

    Le Roman de l'art vivant. Paris: Arthème Fayard, 1959.

FORTUNESCO, Irina ed. *Utrillo.* London: Abbey Library, 1973.

FRANCOLIN, Claude. *La Vie passionnée de Maurice Utrillo.* Paris: Seghers, 1960.

GAUTIER, Maximilien. *Utrillo.* Paris: Le Chêne, 1944.

GORDON, Jan. *Modern French Painters.* London: John Lane, The Bodley Head, 1929.

GROS, Gabriel. *Maurice Utrillo, sa légende.* Lausanne: Marguerat, 1947.

HEUZÉ, Edmond. *Préface de l'Œuvre complet de Maurice Utrillo.* Paris: Pétridès, 1959.

HUYGHE, René. *Les Puissances de l'image.* Paris: Flammarion, 1965.

JAWORSKA, Wladislawa. *Gauguin et l'Ecole de Pont-Aven.* Neuchâtel: Ides et Calendes, 1971.

JOURDAIN, Francis. *Utrillo*. Paris: Braun, 1948. New York: E. S. Herrmann, 1948.

MAC ORLAN, Pierre. *Montmartre, souvenirs*. Brussels: Chabassol, 1946.

Utrillo. Paris: Le Chêne, 1952.

MERMILLON, Marius. *Maurice Utrillo*. Paris: Braun, 1950.

OBERLÉ, Jean. *Utrillo, Montmartre*. Paris: Hazan, 1956.

OLIVIER, Fernande. *Picasso et ses amis*. Paris: Stock, 1933.

PÉTRIDÈS, Paul. *L'Œuvre complet de Maurice Utrillo*. A catalogue raisonné. Paris: Pétridès, 1959–74.

RAYNAL, Maurice. *Anthologie de la peinture en France de 1906 à nos jours*. Paris: Editions Montaigne, 1927. *Modern French Painters*. New York: Brentano's, 1928.

REY, Robert. *Maurice Utrillo, peintre et lithographe*. Paris: Frapier, 1925.

RIBÉMONT-DESSAIGNES, Georges. *Utrillo ou l'enchanteur des rues*. Geneva: Skira, 1948.

ROGER-MARX, Claude. *Maurice Utrillo*. Paris: Flammarion, 1953.

SALMON, André. *L'Air de la Butte*. Paris: La nouvelle France, 1945.

Souvenirs sans fin. Paris: Gallimard, 1956.

Gouaches d'Utrillo. Preface. Paris: Les Quatre Chemins, 1927.

SANTINI. *Modern Landscape Painting*. London: Phaidon Press, 1973.

SLOCOMBE, George. *Rebels of Art. Manet to Matisse*. New York: Robert McBride, 1939.

STORM, John. *The Valadon Drama*. New York: E. P. Dutton, 1959.

TABARANT, Alphonse. *Utrillo*. Paris: Bernheim-Jeune, 1926.

UTRILLO, Maurice. *Autobiographie de Maurice Utrillo, peintre paysagiste*. Unpublished manuscript.

VALORE, Lucie. *Maurice Utrillo, mon mari*. Paris: Forêt, 1956.

VERTEX, Jean. *Le Village inspiré*. Paris: at the author's, 1950.

VLAMINCK, Maurice de. *Portrait avant décès*. Paris: Flammarion, 1943.

VOLLARD, Ambroise. *Souvenirs d'un marchand de tableaux*. Paris: Albin Michel, 1925. *Recollections of a Picture Dealer*. London: Constable, 1936.

WALDEMAR, Georges. *Utrillo*. Paris: Bibliothèque des Arts, 1963. Greenwich, Conn.: New York Graphic Society, 1960.

WARNOD, André. *Les Berceaux de la jeune peinture*. Paris: Albin Michel, 1925.

Les Peintres de Montmartre. Paris: Renaissance du livre, 1928.

Ceux de la Butte. Paris: Julliard, 1947.

Fils de Montmartre. Paris: Fayard, 1955.

Drôle d'époque. Paris: Fayard, 1960.

WEILL, Berthe. *Pan dans l'œil*. Paris: Lipchutz, 1933.

WERNER, Alfred. *Maurice Utrillo*. New York: Abrams, 1981.

YAKI, Paul. *Le Montmartre de nos vingt ans*. Paris: Tallandier, 1933.

ARTICLES IN JOURNALS

BAZIN, Germain. « Utrillo ». *L'Amour de l'Art*, June 1934.

CHANSON, André. « Utrillo ». *Formes*, June 1930.

COLOMBIER, Pierre du. « Utrillo ». *Beaux-Arts*, April 20, 1942.

DORGELÈS, Roland. « La vie dramatique de Maurice Utrillo ». *France-Asie*, January-February 1950.

FELS, Florent. « Utrillo ». *L'Amour de l'Art*, 1963.

JALOUX, Edmond. « Utrillo ». *L'Art et les Artistes*, 1925.

LASSAIGNE, Jacques. « Pro Utrillo ». *L'Art et les Artistes*, 1938.

PARKER, R. A. « A Poet of Old Paris Walls ». *The International Studio*, February 1926.

RAYNAL, Maurice. « Utrillo ». *L'Art d'aujourd'hui*, autumn 1924.

REY, Robert. « Maurice Utrillo ». *L'Amour de l'Art*, 1925.

ROGER-MARX, Claude. « Maurice Utrillo ». *Crapouillot*, No. 9, 1950.

SCHURER, Oskar. « Maurice Utrillo ». *Die Kunst für Alle*, 1926–27, vol. 42, pp. 157-162.

SCIZE, Pierre. « La Croix d'Utrillo ». *Annales politiques et littéraires*, November 1, 1928.

TABARANT, Alphonse. « Critiques ». *L'Œuvre*, January 21, 1921, January 2, 1925.

UTTER, André. « La Carrière de Maurice Utrillo ». *Beaux-Arts*, October 28, 1938.

WARNOD, André. « Maurice Utrillo est mort ». *Le Figaro*, November 7, 1955.

« Maurice Utrillo ». *Comœdia*, December 12, 1922.

« Maurice Utrillo et ses cadets ». *Comœdia*, September 8, 1927.

*Utrillo receives the Legion of Honor
at the Castle of Saint-Bernard
Photograph*

*Utrillo and Lucie Valore
Photograph*

ILLUSTRATIONS

We wish to thank the owners of the pictures reproduced herein, as well as those collectors who did not want their names mentioned. Our special thanks go to the Galerie Schmit and the Galerie Pétridès in Paris, for their kind and valuable assistance.

MUSEUMS

FRANCE

Musée National d'Art Moderne, Paris – Musée d'Art Moderne de la Ville de Paris.

JAPAN

Bridgestone Museum, Tokyo.

SWITZERLAND

Kunsthaus, Zurich.

UNITED KINGDOM

The Tate Gallery, London.

GALLERIES

Acquavella Galleries, New York – Davlyn Galleries, New York – Galerie Walley Findlay, Paris – Galerie Katia Granoff, Paris – Galerie Koller, Zurich – Galerie Daniel Malingue, Paris – Galerie Pétridès, Paris – Galerie Schmit, Paris – Galerie Wildenstein, New York.

PHOTOGRAPHS

Atelier 53, Paris – Atelier 80, Paris – J. M. Canellas, Paris – Service de Documentation Photographique du Musée National d'Art Moderne, Paris – John Webb, London – Photographs of Galerie Schmit: Pages 8, 23, 52, 53, 65, 67, 71, 74, 75, 78, 82.